Nonprofit Quick Guide™

How to Run a Successful Capital Campaign

Linda Lysakowski, ACFRE
Joanne Oppelt, MHA

Nonprofit Quick Guide: How to Run a Successful Capital Campaign

One of the **Nonprofit Quick Guide™** series

Published by Joanne Oppelt Consulting, LLC

ISBN Print Book: 978-1-951978-05-1

13 12 11 10 9 8 7 6 5 4 3 2 1

Printed in the United States of America

About the Authors

LINDA LYSAKOWSKI, ACFRE

Linda is one of approximately one hundred professionals worldwide to hold the Advanced Certified Fundraising Executive designation. She is the author of ten nonfiction books and a contributing author, co-editor, or co-author of eighteen others. She has also written five books in the spiritual and fiction realms.

Linda has more than thirty years in the development field. She worked for a university and a museum before starting her own consulting firm. In her twenty-five years as a philanthropic consultant, Linda has managed capital campaigns that have raised more than $50 million, helped hundreds of nonprofit organizations achieve their development goals, and trained more than forty thousand development professionals in most of the fifty states of the United States as well as in Canada, Mexico, Egypt, and Bermuda.

She served on the Association of Fundraising Philanthropy (AFP) Foundation for Philanthropy Board and on the Professional Advancement Division for AFP. She is a past president of the Eastern Pennsylvania and Sierra (Nevada) AFP chapters. She received the Outstanding Fundraiser of the Year award from the Eastern Pennsylvania, Las Vegas, and Sierra (Nevada) chapters of AFP, was honored with the Barbara Marion Award for Outstanding Service to AFP, and received the Lifetime Achievement Award from the Las Vegas AFP chapter.

Linda is a graduate of Alvernia University with majors in banking and finance as well as theology/philosophy, and a minor in communications. As a graduate of AFP's Faculty Training Academy, she is a Master Teacher.

JOANNE OPPELT, MHA

Joanne, principal of Joanne Oppelt Consulting, LLC, is a seasoned rainmaker with a distinguished track record of success. During her twenty-five-plus years working in the nonprofit arena, she built or rebuilt successful fundraising departments at every stop, helping her organizations grow capacity and more effectively fulfill their missions.

She has held positions from grantwriter to executive director at the nonprofits Community Access Unlimited, Caring Contact: A Listening Community, Family to Family Network of New Jersey, Christian Healthcare Center, March of Dimes Central New Jersey, Prevent Child Abuse New Jersey, and Maternal and Family Health Services. Her extensive background in a variety of work roles and organizations enables her to understand the realities and challenges nonprofit practitioners face–both internally and externally. Her success at every stop positions her to help any nonprofit, whether through her books, trainings, coaching, or consulting practice

Joanne is the author of four books and co-author of six. She has taught at Kean University as an Adjunct Professor in its graduate program. She is also a highly sought-after speaker and presenter.

Joanne holds a master's degree in health administration from Wilkes University, where she graduated with distinction. Her bachelor's degree is in education, with a minor in psychology.

Dedication

This book is dedicated to all the dedicated nonprofit staff who bravely take the big step of a capital campaign, and all the donors who make great things possible in their communities through their leadership gifts to capital campaigns.

Contents

Chapter One

What is a Capital Campaign?

Is a capital campaign different from other fundraising your organization does? Yes, and no!

What's the same? Although many people think capital campaigns are rocket science, when you think of it, rocket science isn't all that much different from the science that makes your car run. The rocket just goes farther and faster. So, you need fuel, an engine, a pilot (or driver), a good navigation system, and probably a lot of things that we don't understand because we are not rocket scientists or automobile designers. But we do know that for all your fundraising, whether it's your annual fund, grants, special events, planned giving, or capital campaigns, there are a few things that are required by all of these fundraising activities:

◆ A strong case for support
◆ Staff support
◆ Board engagement
◆ Volunteers
◆ Donors
◆ A solid plan

So, in many ways, capital campaigns are a lot like the other fundraising activities you're already doing. And, the good thing about a capital campaign is that if you don't already have some of these things in place, putting them in place for the campaign will help strengthen your ongoing fundraising program.

What Makes Capital Campaigns Different?

In most cases, in a capital campaign, the organization raises an amount that is significantly higher than other fundraising they've done in the past.

Like the rocket ship, it's going farther. And like the rocket ship, it's probably going faster—you are dealing with a limited time frame. Unlike grants, events, annual funds, and planned giving, which are perpetual needs in the development office, you may only do one capital campaign in a decade or a lifetime—unless you are in a large organization, such as a university, where capital campaigns seem to be a perpetual occurrence.

One of the biggest differences between a capital campaign and other forms of fundraising is how the donors think about it. Most donors receive your annual appeals and write out a check if they are so inclined. However, with a capital campaign, gifts often come from accumulated assets—perhaps a gift of stock. Capital campaign donors commonly make a multi-year pledge. It's kind of like the way individuals think about their own capital expenditures. When they go to the grocery store or fill up their car's gas tank or charge their car's battery, it is from one pocket—their disposable income. When they buy a house or send kids through college, they typically use a payment plan, take out a loan, or draw on their savings account—a whole different pocket.

Why is it important to understand these similarities and these differences?

First, knowing the similarities might put your mind at ease. If you are following an annual development plan, have a strong case for support, and have support from your staff, board, and volunteers for your ongoing fundraising program, running a capital campaign doesn't sound quite so scary, does it?

However, knowing the important differences, and being prepared to deal with them, will make running a capital campaign less daunting.

Wrapping It Up

◆ Capital campaigns are similar to other fundraising, just on a bigger scale.

◆ It will be important to remember that you are on a timeline with a capital campaign.

◆ Donors think differently about capital campaigns than they do about your ongoing fundraising appeals.

◆ A successful capital campaign will help improve your ongoing development program.

Chapter Two

Are You Ready for a Campaign?

There are several things you should have in place if you're contemplating a capital campaign:

◆ Infrastructure

◆ Staffing

◆ Donors

While some of these can be initiated or improved upon as you begin your campaign, things will move more quickly and smoothly if you have them in place before you start. Your rocket, in other words, will fly farther and faster!

Infrastructure

Infrastructure includes policies and procedures, a good donor tracking system, and a solid case for support.

Why is it important to have fundraising policies in place? Most nonprofit organizations have personnel policies, fiscal policies, and board policies, but these same organizations have often never taken the time to develop fundraising policies. Since you will likely be accepting major donations, gifts in kind, and perhaps unusual gifts, these policies will be especially important during your campaign for several reasons:

◆ They prevent you from accepting gifts that may be inappropriate for your organization or the campaign.

◆ They prevent you from accepting gifts that have "strings" attached to them.

◆ Consistent policies prevent your staff from reinventing the wheel if an unusual situation arises during the campaign.

◆ They provide guidelines for volunteers who are making solicitation calls.
◆ They provide guidelines on how to dispose of or invest non-cash gifts.

Office procedures are essential for all your development activities but will be even more critical during a campaign. This might be the first time you've had to deal with multi-year pledges, major donors, and unusual gifts. You need to be prepared for all these things. Do you have office procedures in place for accepting, recording, and reporting campaign pledges and donations?

What should fundraising policies cover? Some things to consider when developing gift acceptance policies:

◆ How will gifts be solicited?
◆ From whom will the organization accept gifts?
◆ What types of gifts will be accepted?
◆ How will those gifts be acknowledged and recognized?
◆ How will gifts be disposed of or invested?
◆ What kind of stewardship will be provided to the donor?

Do you have gift acceptance policies in place? If not, develop them now!

Part of the infrastructure is having a long-range organizational plan in place. Let's discuss your organization's strategic plan. If you've gone through the strategic planning process recently, the following components are probably in place. If not, you might need to work on your strategic plan. Carefully review the following list and determine what you need to have in place in your organization before you can start to plan a campaign:

◆ We need to update our mission statement.
◆ We need to develop or update our vision statement.
◆ We need to develop or update our values statement.
◆ We need to create or update a strategic plan.
◆ We need a marketing plan.
◆ We need a development plan.
◆ We need to obtain architectural drawings and costs for our project.
◆ We need to develop a preliminary case for support.
◆ We need to conduct a planning (feasibility) study.

Donor Records and Development Office Infrastructure

Having a single database that will track your campaign information, allow you to communicate with your donors and volunteers, and prepare campaign reports, is critical to running a smooth campaign. If you've never run a campaign before, this might be the first time you've had to track multi-year pledges. If you've never worked with volunteer fundraisers, you might not have needed to track the results of volunteer solicitation calls. If you need short-term financing, your lender will want to see cash-flow projections for the campaign. Be sure you have a system that can track these things. How would you rank your organization's giving records?

- ❑ We have a single, integrated, and always-current donor database managed on a computer with development software. This software was purchased within the past three years or is updated regularly and contains complete donor giving histories for the past five years or more.
- ❑ We have reliable individual donors giving records for at least the past three to five years on a computer and are using development software; we can usually produce reports and mailings that meet our needs reasonably well.
- ❑ We have records of almost all individual giving, including most fundraising events, mailings, and activities of the past three years, but they are not integrated using development software. Records are in Excel, Access, or some type of database that is not a licensed fundraising software program.
- ❑ We have almost no permanent records showing gifts received more than about a year ago.

Can you trust that the information in your donor database, including contact information and donation history, is up-to-date and accurate? Will your donor database allow you to record and report on campaign pledges and donations, volunteer activity, and critical donor information?

Planning

Organizational planning is critical. If you don't have solid plans, it will be challenging to attract funders. Remember that while emotion can draw donors to your organization, serious donors want to know that you can deliver on your promises. They want to know that your plan clearly makes sense for your organization *and* for the community. We generally recommended that you have outside facilitators help with strategic planning.

Suppose your campaign involves new construction, expansion of existing facilities, or renovation of an existing building. In that case, you will need to do an architectural study of your existing facilities or have an architect draw up plans for the new building.

If you need to purchase land, you should work with a real estate agent. If you are in the market for land, do you have a professionally developed plan for how much land you need and your requirements (i.e., proximity to bus lines, number of acres, convenient location)?

You also need to prepare a cost budget in consultation with the architect. And you will need a future cash flow projection for lenders to let them know that you will have the funds to pay them back. Your finance officer should be able to give you a cash flow projection.

Staffing

The role of the development staff in your capital campaign should not be underestimated. Although not every organization will have a development staff with campaign experience, it is critical that staff can devote sufficient time to the campaign. If your staff is over-involved in planning and managing special events, writing grant proposals, or involved in non-development activities, such as programs, finance, or public relations, the campaign will suffer.

Let's look at the ability of your staff to launch a campaign. The answers to these questions will help you determine what kind of help you will need from a consultant.

◆ Does your development staff have campaign experience?

◆ How long has your organization's senior development (fundraising) officer been with your organization (in any capacity)?

◆ Have you thought about who will manage the day-to-day campaign operations?

If your development office is staffed by volunteers or is an office with limited staff, you will likely need additional help to manage a capital campaign. Even if you plan to engage a consultant, the campaign will need administrative support. Clerical details that need to be managed include:

◆ Entering pledges and gifts into the database

◆ Researching donor history

◆ Sending meeting notices and minutes to campaign volunteers

◆ Generating campaign reports

◆ Communicating with the staff and volunteers about campaign progress

◆ Preparing campaign materials

◆ Generating direct mail during the later stages of the campaign

◆ If you do not have someone who can handle these tasks, you have several options:

◆ Assign a non-development staff person to do them (who will most likely need some training).

◆ Ask your consultant if they provide support services.

◆ Hire a temporary staff person to help with the campaign.

If you plan to assign a staff person to the campaign, you need to think hard about what you can shift from this person's regular workload. If this staff member is torn between campaign activities and other familiar, more comfortable duties, it is easy to imagine which tasks will be pushed aside! Is your staff over-extended? Rate your development staff's overall ability to meet its existing responsibilities: excellent, good, not very good, no development staff.

Even with a top-notch staff, a consultant is generally engaged to provide the specialized skills a campaign requires. A consultant moves the project along and helps ensure that campaign timelines are met.

The Role of the CEO

Your organization's CEO will have an important role to play in the campaign. In particular, the CEO will need to clear his or her schedule to devote sufficient time to the campaign.

Your CEO must be willing and able to devote sufficient time to the process of identifying, cultivating, and soliciting major donors. It is also vital for the CEO to motivate and inspire campaign leaders. And, of course, the CEO is expected to make an early financial commitment to the campaign, to inspire others to get on board.

How long has your organization's senior executive officer been with your organization (in any capacity)?

If your CEO unexpectedly leaves in the middle of a campaign, the effects can be detrimental. Even if the departure has been planned, it can send the wrong message to your donors. It is critical to have a succession plan in place, and if the departure involves the CEO's termination for cause, a crisis plan might be needed. Answer these questions about the tenure of your CEO:

❑ Our CEO will remain CEO for the duration of the campaign.

❑ Our CEO is likely to retire or leave the organization before this campaign is completed.

❑ We have a succession plan in place if our CEO leaves during the campaign.

Some additional things to ask:

❑ Does your CEO need to be educated in capital campaigns and the role of the CEO in a campaign?

❑ If you asked your CEO to recite your organization's mission statement, how accurate would it be?

❑ How do you perceive the fundraising comfort level of your chief executive officer?

❑ Is your CEO aware of the need for, and committed to, allocating 50 percent or more of his or her workweek to the campaign?

General Staff Engagement

You also need to think about the agency's general staff. Your organization's entire staff should be informed of the campaign early in the planning phase. It will be essential to have your staff support the campaign financially and otherwise, again, to show the community that your organization is *genuinely* committed to this campaign.

If you have not been conducting an annual staff appeal, don't despair—this campaign is a perfect time to introduce staff giving to your organization. Leaders at nonprofits often feel that it is inappropriate to invite the staff to participate financially in fund drives. However, nonprofits employees are generally committed to the organizations for which they work and should be provided an opportunity to show their commitment by participating in campaigns and other fundraising appeals. What percentage of your staff, particularly your senior team, made a financial contribution to your organization last year?

Conducting an ongoing annual staff appeal helps employees feel they are part of your organization's success. It also helps lay the groundwork for a campaign. Offering payroll deductions is a great way to encourage staff members to support your organization.

Donors

In addition to your relationships with your current donors, which are of primary importance during a campaign, your organization's strong awareness within the community is of great benefit. Considering the external factors, such as community awareness and acceptance of your organization, will also be important.

A capital campaign is often the most public type of fundraising your organization will do. While most of the donors to your campaign will be among your loyal supporters, a capital campaign provides you with the optimum opportunity to reach out to the entire community. Many organizations have successfully used a capital campaign to attract new donors to their causes.

Below are some questions to ask about your community. Remember that your community may be local, regional, national, or international. If your campaign will be national or international in scope, you will need to determine the geographic regions where you have large pockets of donors and look at the economic conditions in each of those areas.

♦ Describe the present state of the economy as it is perceived by your major donor prospects.

♦ How well known is your organization within the geographic area in which your program is carried out?

♦ How would you characterize your organization's relationships with local, regional, or national media (whichever is most relevant to your situation)?

♦ Overall, how strong is your organization's website?

Although there is little you can do about the economic climate or even the perception of the economic climate shared by your donors, there are some things you can do to better position your organization within your community. You can strengthen your organization's brand, improve its website, and understand community perceptions of your organization.

Your Organizational Case for Support

An overall agency case for support is what you will use to develop a preliminary capital campaign case statement. Do you have an overall case for support for your organization? If you don't, start one now to have the basis for your campaign case statement.

You will need to test your preliminary case statement before launching your capital campaign with a fully developed case statement. (More about this in **Chapter Four**). Sometimes what *you* might think is important is not what your community members find important. Based on feedback during the study, your case might need to be modified after it's been tested. Your organization's goal might need to be adjusted if the community doesn't think it's realistic.

Competition

Knowing your competition from other nonprofits is also helpful. Although there might be numerous campaigns running simultaneously in your community, not all these will interfere with your campaign. For example, donors might support their church or their university and still be committed to supporting your organization. However, if an organization that is in direct competition with yours is planning a capital campaign, it might be difficult for community members to justify supporting two campaigns for two such organizations.

There might be other fundraising campaigns in your community underway that are likely to approach your best large-gift prospects. How many such campaigns are planned or are presently underway that might be viewed by your prospects as "competing" with your campaign?

List other campaigns that might be happening in your community at the same time you are considering running your campaign. Which of these campaigns might be likely to share your constituency base? What are the start and end dates of these campaigns? How likely is it that your campaign will be significantly affected by this competition?

How Can You Improve Your Organization's Community Awareness?

Before the campaign has been formally announced, publicity should focus on your organization's mission, vision, programs, and accomplishments. Your campaign will be very public after the quiet phase has ended and you hold the public kickoff event. You will want to get as much media coverage as possible for your kickoff event and subsequent campaign announcements and events. We'll talk more about this later.

In both phases, good media relationships are important. Do you have relationships with local media outlets? How strong? Which ones? What local and regional media are important in your community?

Are these media outlets aware of your organization? If not, what strategies can you develop to create more awareness? Here are some examples:

◆ Develop a media kit. Typical media kits contain agency brochures, your agency's case for support, contact information for your organization's media relations person, press releases about your programs, and a list of agency leadership, both staff and board. You should prepare a media kit and deliver it to the media contacts personally, so they know who you are and what your organization does.

◆ List the individual contacts at the various media outlets to whom we need to deliver a media kit.

◆ List the upcoming news and public interest stories (*not* related to your campaign) for which you can develop press releases.

You might have some tremendous human-interest stories about your organization that will attract media attention. For example:

◆ A new law affecting the people you serve could be a reason to write a letter to the editor or invite the media to cover the human side of how this law affects constituents in your community.

◆ A success story about how one of the people you serve overcame the odds to accomplish something amazing could pique the local media's interest. Talking to your program staff or volunteers might uncover some very intriguing success stories, too.

It's time now to develop a plan to get better media coverage. It will be wise to start now to develop a list of issues that affect your industry about which you can write letters to the editor or hold press conferences.

Having good relationships with the media is vital because good media coverage will be critical in getting your message out to potential donors during your campaign. You know you have "arrived" when the media contact *you* for comments on hot issues in your field!

Your Website

It goes (almost) without saying that an effective website is a critical tool for building widespread community awareness. Websites are the primary source of information about a company or organization, and people check an organization's website when they want to learn more about it.

Your website should be interactive and up to date, have a purpose, and provide basic organizational information. One way to evaluate your website is to look at other nonprofit websites, perhaps those of your competitors or organizations like yours in other communities. Make a list of the organizations in your community that seem to be successful at attracting donors. If you are part of a national organization, make a list of those organizations that are the largest or most like yours. Then, set a day aside to research these websites. Use the table below to list the websites you've researched, what you like/don't like about these websites, and what you need to do to improve your website. You can also put bids out to website design firms and see what they have to say about your website. Then incorporate their feedback.

It is crucial that your organization budget for marketing and the technology to support the marketing and development efforts. Does your nonprofit invest in things like computer hardware and software upgrades and updates? Does it employ or engage outside contractors to design professional-looking communications pieces, including your website? Does your organization understand the value of investing in marketing, communications, and appropriate equipment and technology? Presenting a professional image in the community is important is you want to attract new donors.

Wrapping It Up

◆ The more you can improve your infrastructure before you launch your campaign, the faster and farther your "rocket" will fly.

◆ You need to have a suitable donor software system in place to track campaign donations.

◆ Your organization should have a strategic plan and an overall case for support before you start your campaign.

◆ A good website and strong public relations will help you find and attract donors to your campaign.

Chapter Three

What Role Does Your Board Play in a Campaign?

During your feasibility/planning study, which we will be discussing in the next chapter, you may receive recommendations for strengthening or enlarging your board. The board's role will be critical to the success of your campaign. Without a 100 percent commitment from the board, both in concept and financially, it will be impossible to expect others to support this project. Board members are the leaders of your nonprofit. Others will follow their lead.

Many organizations beef up their board's involvement in development efforts before starting campaigns. An organization might expand the board's size, create a development committee, or obtain training and education in fundraising areas for the board. During your planning study, you are likely to receive recommendations for strengthening or enlarging your board.

Some basic questions to ask about your board are:

- ◆ Do your organization's board members attend board and committee meetings regularly?
- ◆ How many of your board members are highly aware of, although perhaps not always in complete agreement with, the organization's mission, programs, history, current challenges, and plans?
- ◆ How many of your board members are comfortably conversant with your organization's mission statement and program?
- ◆ How many of your board members are comfortably conversant with your organization's vision and values statements?

Just as with other the fundraising activities you facilitate, board giving will be a critical first step in your campaign. We've probably all heard board giving defined in terms of the three Gs—Give, Get, or Get off the board. We've often been told that if board members aren't giving and getting, they should leave the board. This concept might seem harsh, and it is not a policy we advocate, but it is important to stress the board's financial commitment before you launch a campaign.

Many funders will not contribute until they know the board has made a financial contribution first. Foundations will often ask this question on the application for a grant. Corporations, businesses, and individuals also want to know that the "family" of the organization has supported it first before asking others to join them in supporting the campaign.

Another way to look at board giving in a more positive light is to consider Linda's "new three Gs" and think about how you can educate, inspire, and improve your board using these concepts. This concept is outlined in detail on our ***Nonprofit Quick Guide: How to Build a Five Star Board.*** In this book, we show you how to get your board members involved in fundraising and making their own commitments to the organization in a way that is best for them.

Here are some questions to get you started in assessing your board:

- ◆ How many board members made a direct financial contribution to your organization last year, beyond buying tickets, purchasing goods, etc.?
- ◆ Beyond their own giving, how many of your board members help raise funds for your organization?
- ◆ How many of your board members can positively influence others in the community who may impact your organization's campaign (e.g., make major financial contributions or provide effective volunteer leadership)?
- ◆ How many of your board members have contacts in the *foundation* world who could help secure grants for your campaign?
- ◆ How many of your board members have contacts in the *business community* who could help secure your campaign's gifts or grants?
- ◆ How many of your board members have contacts with *individual major donors* who could help secure gifts for your campaign?

The chair of your board will play a particularly important role in the campaign. The board chair is typically the official spokesperson for your organization. Without the chair's support and enthusiasm, it will be difficult to convince people that your organization is ready for a campaign. You will want several board members to serve on your campaign cabinet, which we'll discuss in **Chapter Five**, to ensure a good working relationship between the cabinet and the board.

Board/Staff Relations

All organizations have some internal conflict or tension between the board and staff. Board members will not agree on everything (if they do, you probably have a "rubber stamp board"). But meetings and relationships between board and staff members should not be contentious and argumentative. Conflict between the board and the staff can become more apparent during a campaign when so many volunteers are deeply involved with your organization. Volunteers and donors will quickly sense that relationships within the organization are askew and will be reluctant to support the campaign if the conflict is severe. What is the level of conflict in your organization?

Board Education

Building the board's enthusiasm is one of the most critical elements in a capital campaign. But, of course, many of your board members won't think they need *training*! They don't have time for it, and they won't listen to what you say anyway, right?

The first essential step is to avoid the word "training." Many board members don't think they need training but will attend a "Leadership Planning Session," for example. Use a resource, such as my workbook, ***Are You Ready for a Capital Campaign?*** for a board "training session." You can do an all-day or half-day training session for the board before launching a campaign, or do a series of mini-sessions throughout the campaign. If you are working with a consultant, that person can help you plan board training appropriate for your board.

Leading up to the campaign, you can work with the board chair, development committee, or governance committee to plan some type of board education at every board meeting. It can be as simple as fifteen-minute presentations on, say, the "Role of Boards in a Campaign," "Ethical Issues in Capital Campaigns," or "Making the Case for Your Campaign"—you get the idea. For a more intense session, schedule a retreat at a convenient time for most board members, often a Saturday morning or a half-day session in place of, or before, a regular board meeting.

Board education can be done by staff but is usually more effective when done by an outside resource: a consultant, a board member from another organization, or some other experienced person. Outside voices can often tell your board members what they need to hear, with a fresh spin.

Wrapping It Up

- ◆ The board's role in a capital campaign is critical to success.
- ◆ Every board member needs to make a financial contribution to the campaign.
- ◆ Board members should be willing to identify, cultivate, and solicit donors.
- ◆ Several board members should serve on the campaign cabinet.
- ◆ If your board members don't understand their role in a campaign, start the board education process now.

Chapter Four

Do You Need a Planning/Feasibility Study?

In most cases, you will want to do a planning study (sometimes called a feasibility study) before you decide to proceed with a campaign. The study should be done by a consultant to ensure that the interviewed people feel comfortable talking about their perceptions. An experienced consultant will know how to ask the right questions, analyze the interviews' results, and make valid recommendations for your campaign.

A planning study will generally take between three and six months to complete, and the costs will depend on the size of your constituency base, the geographic scope of the study interview process, and other factors. You should expect a full report from the consultant, with recommendations for a campaign goal and timeline, the availability of major donors for your campaign, and any issues that might affect your campaign's success.

Conducting a study will help you prepare for a successful campaign, but it is not the *only* factor determining success. Some questions that will be answered by doing a study include:

- ◆ The likelihood that the goal can be reached
- ◆ An analysis of donor availability, identifying who will support the project at the necessary levels
- ◆ The availability of leadership-level volunteers to serve on the campaign cabinet
- ◆ The public's perception of your case for support and the plans presented in it

During this study, the people to be interviewed will usually be major donors to your organization and those you feel could be. They will also be those with broad community connections who might be willing to serve on the campaign cabinet.

Before engaging a consultant to do the study, you should attempt to determine who you will ask the consultant to interview. Most consultants will want to interview between thirty and fifty people. If your campaign is larger in size and scope, this number could be greater. Not all of the people on your list will be available for an interview, so you should start with a list of seventy-five to one hundred people. The list will then be divided into an A list, a B list, and a C list. A-list people are those who *must* be interviewed, B-list individuals are those who *should* be interviewed, and the C-list contains the names of those who *could* be interviewed. Answering this question will help determine how ready you are to create a list of people who should be interviewed.

Regarding the list of possible interviewees:

- ❏ We have developed a list of people to be interviewed during the study. There are _____ (number of people) on this list.
- ❏ We do not have a list developed but can put one together fairly quickly.
- ❏ We have no idea whom we should plan to interview and will need some guidance from the consultant in this regard.

Engaging a Consultant for the Study

The study should always be done by an outside consultant, knowledgeable about capital campaigns and studies, who does not come into the process with preconceived notions about potential success or failure, and can comfortably interview prospective donors and volunteers.

Usually, the consultant will also prepare the preliminary case statement and begin with an internal assessment of your readiness to conduct a campaign, as covered in **Chapter Two**.

If you have not yet identified a consultant for the study, how will you go about this process?

- ❏ We have identified a consultant who will perform the study.
- ❏ We have identified several firms/consultants to be interviewed.
- ❏ We will ask for written proposals from these consultants and have assigned someone responsible for developing the request for proposal (RFP), reviewing these proposals, and making recommendations to the board.

We generally recommend doing a planning study before the campaign. This grid will help you develop a plan to do the study:

Planning Study Task	Budget	Person or Team Responsible	Timeline to Complete
Determine the need for study			
Establish the goals of the study			
Develop a list of consultants to be considered			
Develop RFP			
Distribute RFP			
Select consultants to be interviewed			
Interview consultants			
Select consultant			
Sign contract			

That said, there may be some instances where a study is not necessary before launching a campaign. Usually, a study is not needed when:

◆ The campaign goal is small, and your annual giving results indicate that the goal would be easily reached.

◆ You have recruited a campaign cabinet of community leaders whose support assures success.

◆ You have financial commitments for leadership gifts that total at least two-thirds of the campaign goal.

◆ Time constraints do not allow for a delay in starting the campaign.

◆ You have good community awareness and support for your case.

◆ You are internally ready for the campaign.

Unless you are reasonably confident that you can reach your goal, enlist the support of volunteers who will work on the campaign and have a strong sense of your donor support.

Wrapping It Up

◆ You will most likely want to conduct a planning (feasibility) study to assess both your internal readiness for a campaign and the community's willingness and ability to support this campaign.

◆ The study should be conducted by an outside consultant who will have the skills, experience, and expertise to develop the questions to be asked, interview prospective donors, analyze the interview results, and make recommendations for your campaign.

◆ You can facilitate the study process by assembling the material needed for the case for support and a list of people to be interviewed.

◆ You may not need a study if you are confident of success, but we recommend a study in most cases.

Chapter Five

The Role of the Campaign Cabinet and Committees

In our opinion, volunteer campaign leadership is the single most important factor in campaign success. The right campaign chair can inspire volunteers, donors, board members, and staff. Volunteers bring to the table contacts, cash, and clout. Choose your volunteer leadership wisely because volunteers can make or break your campaign.

Campaign Leadership

It will be vital to recruit a potential campaign chair or co-chairs with all the following qualities:

◆ Passion for your cause and organization

◆ Willingness to make a leadership gift or one that will stretch the individual's normal giving pattern

◆ Positive influence with people of wealth

◆ Time to devote to the campaign

◆ Leadership skills

Sometimes campaign leadership is recruited too early because organizations want to get moving with the campaign. Caution: think through who would make the best chair for your campaign. Review the list of qualities above and then determine whether:

◆ You have identified one or more people who have all these qualities. They have agreed to serve in this capacity.

◆ You have identified one or more people who have most or all these qualities but have not yet asked these people to serve in this capacity.

◆ You have not yet identified anyone with either most or all these qualities.

◆ You have already asked someone who possesses some, but not all, of these qualities to serve as your campaign chair.

In addition to the campaign chair (or chairs), you will need a campaign cabinet, usually about twenty-five to thirty people. It will consist of the chairs of each of the divisions you've identified as part of the campaign. Although the committees will vary depending on your organization, typically there are these committees:

◆ Leadership Gifts Committee—a small group of people who will identify and solicit leadership gifts (the amount of a leadership gift to be determined by your table of gifts).

◆ Major Gifts Committee—a small group that will identify and solicit the next tier of donors. Sometimes in a small campaign, this role might be combined with the Leadership Gifts Committee.

◆ A Foundation Gifts Committee—if there are several foundation funders you plan to approach, these would be people with contacts in local, regional, or national foundations.

◆ A Business Gifts Committee—responsible for identifying and soliciting local and regional businesses.

◆ Committees based on your organization's needs, i.e., alumni gifts, parent gifts, regional committees (if your organization is statewide, national, or international in scope).

◆ Phone appeal and mail appeal committees, whose work comes at the tail end of the campaign.

Also, there may be various committees that are not involved in direct solicitation, such as:

◆ Prospect Identification Committee
◆ Cultivation Committee
◆ Stewardship and Recognition Committee
◆ Finance and Budget Committee (unless this is being handled internally with staff)
◆ Publicity Committee (also sometimes handled internally by PR staff)
◆ Event Committees—to handle kickoff event, groundbreaking, dedication, and open house activities

Recruiting and Working with Capital Campaign Volunteers

Capital campaign volunteers are a critical component of a successful campaign. So, where do you find these volunteers, and how do you manage the process? The names acquired during the planning study are an excellent place to start. You can begin by recruiting campaign cabinet members who displayed an interest in the project or were suggested by interviewers. Then add to the list of potential volunteers through strategy meetings with the board, staff, and consultants.

Remember that the campaign chair, co-chairs, or office of the chair is *the most* critical role in the campaign. This person or persons must be selected carefully and should be able to inspire, motivate, and lead the rest of the campaign cabinet to success. Here are some steps to follow in recruiting volunteer leadership for your campaign:

◆ Always have a job description for every volunteer.

◆ Develop the job description *first* and then find the right person to fill each role.

◆ Once the job descriptions are in place, and a list of potential volunteers to fill each position is in place, develop a volunteer recruitment packet with the job description, the campaign timeline, the campaign organizational chart, the case for support, and other pertinent information about the organization and the campaign.

◆ Select the campaign cabinet members and provide them with suggestions for volunteers for their committees based on suggestions received in the planning study, from the strategy sessions, and from other cabinet members.

◆ Hold regularly scheduled campaign cabinet meetings at times and locations that are convenient for most of the cabinet members. Meetings are usually monthly unless your campaign will run three years or more, in which case you might opt for bi-monthly or quarterly cabinet meetings.

◆ Insist on training and ongoing report meetings for volunteers who will solicit donors during the period in which these volunteers will be actively soliciting for the campaign.

◆ Provide a fundraising mentor for committee members who are newer at fundraising.

◆ Stay in close contact with volunteers through emails, text messages, online meetings such as Zoom, and phone calls to update them on campaign news, inquire about their calls' status, and inform them of anything that causes a change in the campaign plan.

◆ Set up a special website page just for campaign volunteers to stay on top of campaign development conveniently and throughout the campaign.

It will usually take hundreds of volunteers to run a capital campaign unless your campaign is small or narrowly focused. You will need a job description for each of these volunteers, and you will need to provide campaign training for them. The training will be based on their role in the campaign. For example, the Leadership Gifts Committee would receive training to ask for major gifts; the Phonathon Volunteers will need training in asking for smaller donations over the phone. All volunteers will need to be shown how to become familiar with and articulate the case.

Wrapping It Up

◆ Volunteers are often the most critical aspect of a successful campaign.

◆ Choosing the right chair is the first step in ensuring success.

◆ A campaign cabinet must have the right people for each committee.

◆ Develop a volunteer recruitment packet with all the vital components, especially a job description for every volunteer.

Chapter Six

Developing Your Campaign Plan

You've come this far—have done a study or determined that you don't need one, and feel ready to launch a campaign. What's next?

Once the staff has agreed this campaign is needed, you will want to get the approval to launch a campaign from your board of directors.

Then you need a campaign plan. You need to think about your campaign's timeline, the budget, and how the campaign will fit into your overall development program. Your campaign plan will include an organizational chart showing the divisions determined to be needed for your campaign. It will also include job descriptions for all the volunteers you will involve in the campaign, a donor recognition plan, a publicity plan, and a plan to identify and cultivate donors in each division (more about this in the next chapter).

Campaign Budget

How large a budget for campaign expenses have you included as part of your total campaign goal? Campaign costs typically run anywhere from 8 to 12 percent of your overall goal. Many factors affect the costs of your campaign. For example:

◆ Whether you're using campaign counsel, how much support you need from counsel, and whether the counsel is local, regional, or national

◆ Whether you need to hire additional staff to support the campaign management

◆ Whether your campaign is national or international in scope and how much travel it will require
◆ How long the campaign will run

Almost every organization that plans a capital campaign engages a consultant to help. While hiring a consultant isn't an absolute guarantee of success, it can help overcome some campaign roadblocks. For example, a consultant can:

◆ Ensure that staff members stay focused on campaign activities
◆ Develop a plan for recruiting and educating campaign volunteers
◆ Provide the expertise to plan and execute a campaign
◆ Write a compelling case for support

This is in addition to the costs of a consultant to provide the internal and external assessment of your chances for success through the study discussed in **Chapter Four**.

The cost of hiring a consultant will depend on the firm's size and location, the degree of experience the consultant assigned to your campaign has, and the amount of time the consultant will need to spend on your campaign. If your budget is limited and you can't afford a consultant on a retainer basis, our advice is to engage a consultant to do the planning study to determine the likelihood of a successful campaign and draft the campaign plan—the roadmap for conducting a successful campaign. Often you will be able to implement the plan with minimal support for the consultant if you have experienced staff. And, you might consider engaging a campaign manager as a temporary or part-time staff person, especially if your staff is already overburdened.

Other things you will need to budget for are meeting expenses, postage, travel expenses (especially if your campaign will be national or regional in scope), recognition items, promotional materials such as brochures, videos, webpages, and the like.

Most often, the campaign budget is included in the overall campaign goals. Most donors understand that you need to invest money to raise money, especially in a capital campaign.

Timeline

Most campaigns will take at least eighteen months to two years to complete, but again, the answer to how long your campaign will run is ... it depends.

It depends on your campaign's financial goal, how many leadership gifts prospects you have, and the geographic scope of your campaign.

Other factors that impact the timeline include the recruitment of volunteer leadership and staff availability. And don't forget—you need to add time for planning, time to conduct a study, and possible delays in getting permits, purchasing land, and securing architectural plans. And, especially if you don't have a strong fundraising program in place, you will need time to identify and cultivate donors.

Plan B: What If We're Not Ready?

If you find that your organization is ready, this book is designed to provide you with the guidance you need to run a successful campaign.

But what if, after reading this book, doing some honest self-assessment, or conducting a planning study, you've determined that your organization is not ready for a campaign now, is all lost?

No!

This book will still provide you with the tools to help strengthen your organization for a future campaign.

But what if you need the space, the equipment, or the renovations *now*? What if you *can't* wait? There are some other options you can consider:

- Running a campaign in phases, addressing the most critical needs first
- Financing your project through a line of credit or other short-term financing
- Delaying the expansion of your program until you can build the required facilities or provide the equipment needed for these services
- Collaborating with another nonprofit to provide the services you would provide in an expanded space

A phased campaign is often the answer. The advantages of this approach are twofold: you can bite off a manageable chunk of the campaign. Often, a successful small campaign will help you prepare for a more comprehensive campaign later. The disadvantage is that you can end up in a perpetual campaign mode, which sometimes leads to staff, volunteer, and donor fatigue. However, if you time your campaign right and make it clear from the beginning that you are running a phased campaign, this approach can be ideal.

Obtaining a loan to build or renovate is also often a good approach. Don't go into this plan with the idea that later, when you are ready, you will run a debt-reduction campaign. It's hard to raise money for debt reduction; most debt reduction campaigns are not successful because donors think you didn't plan well if you expanded programs and services when you couldn't afford to do so. Sometimes debt reduction can be included in a larger campaign as part of the project. For example, you might try to raise $1 million to pay off existing debt while raising $8 million for a new expansion.

As hard as it is to delay your program's expansion because you simply are not ready for a campaign, sometimes waiting is the only answer. Engage your organization in a strategic planning process to determine whether the programs are really needed, and then if they are, see if there is some other channel of delivery. If the programs are genuinely time-critical, you might need to lease space or collaborate with another organization to provide immediate program delivery before you can house them yourself.

If you are not ready for a campaign, go back and reread this book, get *Are You Ready for a Capital Campaign?* Do the homework in it. Review what you've learned about the importance of board commitment, staffing infrastructure, public awareness, donor prospects, and volunteer involvement. These are usually areas where most organizations find their weaknesses. See what you can do in these areas to strengthen your organization.

Even if you decide not to launch a campaign, strengthening your organization in these areas will help you become stronger in the long run and increase your annual giving. Who knows? You might even find that you can raise enough money in your annual giving program to fund some of the capital expenses you need to expand your program.

Wrapping It Up

◆ Don't try to jump into the campaign without a solid plan in place.
◆ Your campaign plan should include a campaign organizational chart and job descriptions for all staff, volunteers, and consultants during the campaign.
◆ A realistic timeline is critical.
◆ The budget for the campaign needs to be in the campaign plan.
◆ Your plan should also include a Plan B, in case you are not ready to launch the campaign yet.

Chapter Seven

Finding and Soliciting Donors

Ah, donors! Without them, no campaign can succeed. They are a big part of the fuel that launches your rocket ship. So, do you already have loyal donors, and will they step up and support this campaign? Do you have prospects for the leadership gifts needed to ensure success? Will this campaign help you attract new donors? Hopefully, these questions have been answered during your planning study.

If you find that your organization has difficulty attracting a particular category of donors—individual major donors, foundations, organizations, or businesses—you might want to plan some special cultivation events and activities to build relationships with these donors.

You will need to determine which are the best activities or events to attract donors, while at the same time not over-taxing your budget.

For example, if you seek to build relationships with the business community, a business leader's breakfast might be a good event for you to consider. If, on the other hand, you want to build more awareness among major individual donors, you might plan a series of intimate cocktail parties in board members' or other volunteers' homes. Or you might want to meet with these donors one-on-one or invite them for a tour of your organization. Use a table to create a donor cultivation plan: under the first column, list the types of donors you need to cultivate—foundations, businesses, organizations, and individual donors. Then add columns for the types of events and activities you will use to cultivate this segment, who will be responsible for the development of a cultivation plan for that event or activity, how much it will cost, and the timeline for each event or activity. You can learn more about this process in our book, *Nonprofit Quick Guide: How to Run a Successful Cultivation Event.*

You might need to develop some materials, events, or activities to improve donor awareness and donor relations. Develop a grid to help you plan accordingly. Some programs and materials you might add to your list include developing an annual report or a newsletter, conducting "thank-a-thons," sending personal notes, developing a social media program, developing and distributing media kits and media releases, improving your website, visiting major donors personally, and holding cultivation events for various segments of your population. Be sure to assign costs, persons responsible, and timelines for each of these undertakings.

How Important is the Table of Gifts in a Campaign/Appeal?

In a capital campaign, the table of gifts is a critical first step and should be part of your support case. The table of gifts is important to help keep staff and volunteers focused on the fact that leadership and major gifts are the lifeblood of any fundraising campaign. Without those gifts, no capital campaign can succeed. The internal table of gifts should also show how many prospects you will typically need to secure those major gifts, as in the example below:

Internal Table of Gifts for $7.5 Million Campaign Goal

Committee	Number of prospects needed	Number of gifts needed	At the following levels	Total
Leadership Gifts	3	1	$2,000,000	$ 2,000,000
	9	3	500,000	1,500,000
	15	5	250,000	1,250,000
Major Gifts	30	10	100,000	1,000,000
	36	12	50,000	600,000
	45	15	25,000	375,000
Other Gifts	54	18	15,000	270,000
	60	20	10,000	200,000
	Many	Many	Under $10,000	120,000
Total				$7,500,000

Does this table of gifts get shared with your donors and prospects? Yes! In fact, it should be shared with the interviewees during a planning (or feasibility) study. It is important to show prospective donors that you need those big gifts and a lot of smaller gifts for your campaign to succeed. In your preliminary case for support and the final one, you will eliminate the "number of prospects needed" column as this is only important for the staff and volunteers who will be raising the money. Your case might show a table like this:

Table of Gifts for $7,500,000 Campaign Goal

Number of gifts needed	At the following levels	Total
1	$2,000,000	$ 2,000,000
3	500,000	1,500,000
5	250,000	1,250,000
10	100,000	1,000,000
12	50,000	600,000
15	25,000	375,000
18	15,000	270,000
20	10,000	200,000
Many	Under $10,000	120,000
		$7,500,000

Remember, it is important to show this reality to donors and volunteers to dispel thoughts such as, "if we can get a thousand donors to give us $1,000, we will make our $1 million goal."

By the way, some people think that a table of gifts is only important in a capital campaign. But all of your fundraising efforts should be focused on the *90 to 95 percent of your gifts come from 5 to 10 percent of your donors.* Something to think about!

Solicitation

The solicitation process and timing need to be outlined carefully in your campaign plan. Start with the number of prospects you have identified in each of the divisions of your campaign. Next, recruit the number of volunteers needed in each division, using the five-to-one rule for leadership and major gifts, and any gifts that will be solicited in person. No volunteer should be assigned more than five prospects to solicit. In the later phases of the campaign, where you might be doing telephone solicitations, callers can usually complete about thirty calls during one shift on the phones.

Be sure to carefully select the right solicitor to call on the right donor—someone the donor knows and trusts is usually the most effective "asker." All staff and volunteers must be trained in making calls, from the top leadership gifts down to the volunteer who will make phone calls. There are tons of books out there on asking and receiving major gifts, so we won't belabor the point here. But it is crucial that anyone involved in making major gift calls can understand and articulate the case, knows how to listen to the donors, understands the options available as presented in the case, and has made their own gift first.

Donor Stewardship and Recognition

It has been said that good stewardship is the last step in the first gift and the first step in getting the next gift. Stewardship includes ensuring that:

- ◆ The donor's best interests are the primary consideration;
- ◆ The organization conforms to all applicable laws;
- ◆ All fundraising is done with the highest ethical standards; and
- ◆ The organization develops proper systems of acknowledgment and recognition for the donor.

Donors should never be persuaded to contribute to a cause they don't fully support or make a gift that may not be in their own best interest. The Association of Fundraising Professionals (AFP) provides a Code of Ethical Standards that serves as a guide for its members but can provide a solid ethical basis for all fundraisers. In addition to this code, numerous other professional organizations have similar codes of ethics.

Some common issues that appear in all these codes are that fundraisers, either staff or consultants, should never work on a percentage-based fee, that fundraisers must be open and honest about the organization and its mission, and that fundraisers will always conform to legal requirements regarding the solicitations, recording, use, and acknowledgment of gifts.

In addition to these codes of ethics, a Donor Bill of Rights is also available on AFP's website. This bill of rights informs the donors of things they are entitled to when making a nonprofit gift. For example, donors have the right to know who is on the organization's governing board; to know whether the person soliciting them is a professional counsel, paid staff, or a volunteer; and to remain anonymous in their giving, among other things. We encourage you to promote this bill of rights and adhere to its principles.

Other important aspects of all fundraising that must be considered during a campaign are the IRS's legal requirements and other regulatory agencies, such as state and local municipalities that may govern fundraising activities. For example, most states regulate fundraising activities by requiring nonprofit organizations, fundraising counsel, and professional solicitors to register before conducting fundraising campaigns. Your organization should be aware of its own state's requirements and other states' requirements in which you may plan to solicit.

You also need to be sure that a paid consultant or professional solicitor is registered within the state if required to do so. IRS requirements regarding "quid pro quo" contributions, the fair market value of consideration given to donors, and statements for donations over $250 must be followed in the recording and acknowledgment of gifts. For information on state requirements, contact your department of state. Your accounting or auditing firm, or a lawyer, can give advice and counsel regarding IRS regulations. *(This book is not meant to provide legal or accounting advice. Please contact appropriate counsel for this advice.)*

Acknowledging Donations

Acknowledgment of donors' gifts should always be done promptly. Sending a thank-you letter within twenty-four hours of receiving their gift is recommended. All donors should be acknowledged with a personal letter of thanks, regardless of the size of their gift.

It is said that a donor should be thanked seven times for a gift before asking for the next donation. While you would not want to send seven thank-you letters, there are other ways to thank the donor. A personal phone call from the campaign volunteer who solicited the gift, a handwritten note from the executive director or chair of the board, a phone call from a program recipient—all can do wonders to bond the donor to your organization. And of course, the formal receipt with the IRS statement stating that no goods or services were received in consideration of this donation can be considered another form of thanking the donor.

Recognition is another facet of thanking the donor for their gift. Recognition can come in many forms. Listing donors in the organization's newsletter or annual report, issuing a press release about a major gift, donor walls, bricks, and personal mementos given to the donors are all ways of providing donor recognition. Special recognition events at which donors are publicly recognized for their contributions can also be effective.

Remember, however, that some donors wish to remain anonymous, and their anonymity must always be ensured. Providing a place on the pledge card or letter of intent for donors to print their name exactly the way they wish to be recognized, and a box where they can check if they want to remain anonymous, are simple ways of ensuring that donor recognition will be done according to the donor's wishes. A good software system (discussed in an earlier chapter) will also provide the means to track this information when preparing the recognition items. Of course, these pledge forms and software systems must be in place at the start of the campaign, so recognition must be considered before the campaign begins and be a part of the campaign plan and budgeted for, not decided at the end of the campaign when it is time to recognize donors.

Named gifts are important during a capital campaign. Offering donors the option to name a building, a room, a program, or items such as benches and trees, often inspires donors to make a stretch gift to name something near and dear to them, their company or foundation, or a loved one.

Besides adhering to legal and ethical standards, the organization benefits from good stewardship in other ways. Professional staff will feel more confident knowing they are acting according to the highest professional standards, and donors feel more confident knowing the organizations they support follow good stewardship practices. Many an organization has been the beneficiary of a huge estate gift because it provided good stewardship of the donor's smaller gifts.

Wrapping It Up

◆ The table of gifts is important to show donors that leadership gifts are critical, but all gifts are meaningful.

◆ If you haven't identified enough prospective donors, you may need to spend more time identifying and cultivating donors.

◆ Start by dividing your prospects into the division in which they are likely best suited and recruit the right volunteers and staff to solicit each donor prospect.

◆ Donor recognition and stewardship are critical.

◆ Respect a donor's choice to remain anonymous.

Chapter Eight

What Happens When Things Go Wrong

Capital campaigns often start with early excitement, enthusiasm, and momentum. But sometimes, especially with a five-year or longer campaign timeline, this enthusiasm wanes. When a campaign loses momentum or is perceived to lose momentum, you may be facing a stalled campaign. Whether your stalled campaign is due to a lack of planning or from unforeseen external circumstances, use this opportunity to re-plan, regroup, and re-energize staff and volunteers.

Why Do Campaigns Stall?

Campaigns can stall for many reasons. It could be due to a lack of prospects—a lack of well-cultivated major donors. Many campaigns stall because organizations weren't prepared when they started. They didn't have community backing, or they didn't have board support, or they didn't have the infrastructure in place.

Other factors affecting momentum include a weak or poorly articulated case, leadership issues, little or no planning, or timing issues. An economic downturn can also initiate a stall, as in the Great Recession of 2008 where many campaigns had to suddenly deal with a delayed number of commitments and pledge fulfillment.

Many nonprofits go into campaigns with a great deal of hope but very little planning. If you struggle to meet your annual goals, it may be even harder to find the time and focus on doing serious strategic planning.

Lack of Prospective Donors

A shallow prospect pool tends to be an issue for smaller organizations without a fulltime ongoing major gift operation. These nonprofits may not have a history of well-cultivated major donors who know about their organization. Typical major gift cultivation takes eighteen months to three years. If you haven't done a good job building relationships, you are missing the boat! It is almost impossible to get a major gift from someone who is not familiar with or has no passion for your organization.

The Board's Role

Another stumbling block for campaigns is not having engaged, energized, and committed leadership. The board needs to be on the front line of marketing and donor cultivation. We've found that with a failing campaign, it's usually because the board isn't behind it. You can't run a successful campaign without the board's commitment. Until 100 percent of the board gives, you can't go out and ask for community support.

The Value of Volunteers

If you don't have enough volunteers, or they're not properly coached or trained, then you're at risk for a stalled campaign. Volunteers must be trained to avoid common missteps, such as asking too early, not asking for enough, over-cultivating, or simply not asking for a gift.

In our experience, volunteer leadership can be the most critical aspect of success. Perhaps you haven't recruited the right volunteers, or maybe a key leader resigns in the middle of a campaign. You can avoid this by having a vice-chair or even three co-chairs. Co-chairs should have complementary skills. For example, the chair might be visionary and good at planning, while the co-chair might be better at making the ask.

The Case for Support

A case for support that is not compelling enough to motivate gifts may make it difficult to get your campaign moving. Donors and prospects outside of your "family" need to understand that your organization fills a real need in your community, that you are uniquely positioned to provide the necessary help, and that their participation in a successful campaign will make the community a better place. Asking for gifts because you need the money is not the right approach—what nonprofit doesn't need money? As we've said earlier, everyone who's asking for gifts on your behalf needs to be able to articulate the case for support. They need to demonstrate to prospective donors that your organization plays a crucial role and explain how this campaign helps people in your community.

Timing

Campaigns can also stall due to doing steps out of order, such as launching a campaign with a direct mail effort, which usually comes last. We've had direct experience with this when "rescuing" a stalled campaign advised by a consultant that did not have capital campaign experience. Another mistake we've seen is publicly announcing a campaign too early, such as announcing a $1.5 million campaign after raising only $32,000—the huge gap between commitments and the goal raised questions about this campaign's credibility. In either case, you can start over and re-launch with a more effective plan.

Getting Back on Track

A stalled campaign needs new energy to get it back on track. Take time out to evaluate your campaign's strengths and weaknesses and plan and implement the changes necessary to restore campaign credibility internally and externally. If your campaign was under-planned, this is the time to take inventory of your fundraising fundamentals and create a plan to restore momentum. If your leadership is burned out, now is the time to create a plan to attract fresh energy.

As we've already mentioned, if you can't afford to hire a consultant to be with you every step of the way, hire one in the beginning and let them do the planning with you. If you have a good campaign plan, you can implement a lot of it yourself without getting stuck along the way. Usually, you need a campaign planning study, or you need more time to research and cultivate donors if you're not going to do a study.

A campaign planning study, done before a campaign is launched, helps assess your campaign readiness and is also an effective early cultivation opportunity. This is that stage where you can identify and cultivate your leading donors and determine whether, as a group, their gift capacity and connection to your organization are strong enough to fulfill your goal. If you haven't done a study, or don't have a solid campaign plan in place, get the help you need and do it now!

Jump-start Your Campaign Leadership

Board members who aren't interested in fundraising often leave during a campaign. So, at some point, you need to be prepared to find new board members who will work for you. An effective board nominating process will help you assemble a board that will move you towards your goal.

Internally, campaign leadership generally falls on the executive director. If the executive director does not understand or accept this role, ask your consultant to explain it to them. Sometimes the executive director doesn't want a front-line fundraising role for various reasons, such as personality or health. Can the development director substitute for the executive director? It is usually a challenge, but we've seen it work.

And of course, if volunteer leadership is faltering, replace the campaign chair.

Get Someone to Challenge Donors

Linda worked on a close-to-the-finish campaign, but they couldn't get the last quarter-million dollars—the amount they needed to start construction. So, the campaign implemented a challenge grant by going back to a top donor and asking him to consider an additional gift in the form of a challenge gift. Through this challenge grant, they met their goal by going back to donors for a second ask. They were able to raise that money because they got people to either extend their pledges for an extra year or got them to increase the amount based on the challenge grant.

It is often successful to encourage donors through a challenge grant from a well-known donor or a highly known and respected foundation. It's like a seal of approval on your organization and on your campaign, and some people are influenced by that. They want to invest in a winner. Some foundations like to make the capstone gift to help nonprofits sprint to their campaign finish line.

Motivation is the most important element in a campaign, and a challenge grant has a powerful effect on motivation. The inherent urgency of a challenge is a good inducement to get in front of donors who have pending proposals. A challenge grant can motivate your volunteer solicitors. For example, if you have a volunteer committed to cultivating five major prospects, the volunteer may not have a sense of urgency with a five-year timeline. The challenge grant helps motivate them to get started with their prospects sooner.

The best prospects for a challenge grant are those who have already made a commitment to the campaign. We find that donors who already gave will often agree to do more when the urgency is conveyed properly. Maybe they gave you less than what you asked for the first time, or their capacity to give may have improved.

Wrapping It Up

◆ Sometimes campaigns falter due to things out of your control, such as the economy.

◆ More often, stalled campaigns result from a lack of planning. Stop and take the time to plan.

◆ If leadership falters during a campaign, replace the campaign chair, or promote a vice-chair to the chair's position.

◆ If staffing is lacking, hire a temporary or part-time staff person.

◆ Re-evaluate your case for support.

◆ Consider a challenge grant.

Chapter Nine

Bringing It All Together

We've covered everything from getting ready for a campaign, doing an internal assessment, and conducting a planning study to planning your campaign, finding the right volunteer leaders for your campaign, and identifying, cultivating, soliciting, and stewarding donors. We've even talked about what to do to jump-start a stalled campaign.

Some key points to remember are:

◆ Ensure you have the infrastructure in place—a good software system, policies and procedures, and board approval to proceed with a campaign.

◆ Beef up your staff, if necessary, and make sure everyone understands what their role will be in the campaign.

◆ Engage an outside consultant to do a planning/feasibility study.

◆ Have all your architectural plans and costs laid out, including land options.

◆ Create a compelling case statement, laying out options for the donor to participate at every level.

◆ Create a detailed campaign plan, including timeline, budget, and job descriptions for all volunteers.

◆ Recruit a top-notch campaign chair and campaign cabinet.

◆ Train volunteers, staff, and board in every aspect of the campaign they will be involved in.

We feel it is important to plan for your organization's life *after* a campaign. If your organization has run a capital campaign in the past, you will want to draw on that experience. Too often, organizations fail to keep campaign donors and volunteers involved in ongoing development efforts. If you've had experience with past campaigns, you can often reengage volunteers and donors in this and future campaigns. What has been your organization's experience with a major fundraising campaign? How successful was your organization's last major fundraising campaign? Do you have records from past campaigns that include donors, volunteers, staffing, and consultants?

Life After the Campaign

Once your campaign is over and before the glow of success fades, you should think about how your organization can "capitalize" on its success to build a stronger development program and a stronger organization for the future.

One of the major benefits of a successful campaign is that it leaves an organization much stronger than before. The reasons for this are:

◆ The campaign starts with an internal assessment, and that assessment will result in recommendations to strengthen your organization's infrastructure.

◆ Increased public relations efforts during a campaign result in a heightened awareness of the organization in the community.

◆ Volunteer involvement in the campaign provides future volunteer fundraisers for the organization's ongoing development efforts.

◆ Your staff benefits from working with a consultant and gains knowledge and experience, which are assets to them and the organization.

So, make sure you retain good records of donations, volunteers, and staff strengths and weaknesses. Debrief with the campaign chairs often during the campaign and after, so you can be better prepared for your next campaign—and, more importantly, so you can strengthen your ongoing development program.

9781951978051